PEAK VILLAGES

Photography by KAREN FRENKEL
Words by ROLY SMITH

HALSGROVE

First published in 2002 by Halsgrove
Text © 2002 Roly Smith
Images © 2002 Karen Frenkel

British Library Cataloguing-in-Publication Data
A CIP record for this title is available from the British Library

ISBN 1 84114 185 2

HALSGROVE

Halsgrove House
Lower Moor Way
Tiverton, Devon EX16 6SS
Tel: 01884 243242
Fax: 01884 243325
email: sales@halsgrove.com
website: www.halsgrove.com

Printed and bound in Italy
by Centro Grafico Ambrosiano

Contents

PHOTOGRAPHER'S ACKNOWLEDGEMENTS

I would like to thank all those kind and patient villagers and general 'passers by' who helped me in so many different ways while I was taking the photographs for this book. Whether it was to act as willing models, make me cups of tea, tell me interesting stories about their village, allow me into their gardens or just give me general advice – it has all been very much appreciated. I would also like to thank my family and friends for being so patient and understanding over the final couple of months while meeting the deadline.

PHOTOGRAPHER'S NOTES

When I first agreed to do this book I certainly underestimated the difficulties which I would encounter. The major one was trying to cover over 60 villages in a short period of time, summing each one up in one or two shots which wouldn't soon be out of date. One thing which was clear on visiting them all was how much things were constantly changing. Many images taken a few years ago were now out of date, whether it was new extensions being erected, major renovations, shops and businesses changing names – or even disappearing altogether and being converted back to accommodation. Indeed, by the time this book is published there will be further changes again, I'm sure.

After initial reconnoitres in early March, it soon became evident that it was necessary to visit most of the villages on numerous occasions at different times of day and different times of the month to capture the best lighting conditions, together with prominent trees, flowers or shrubs which would enhance the pictures.

This resulted in a very complicated list of where to be and when, and fitting this around the stormy weather which we had in 2002 resulted in a rather daunting task. Some villages required visits very early in the morning or very late in the evening for the best lighting, so many miles were covered flitting from one place to the next from my complicated list. Often this was undertaken only to find that on arrival at my pre-planned destination, scaffolding had been erected or the road was being dug up, never mind the usual cars, lorries and vans all being parked in the way. This would result in a change of plan and yet another visit. Once photos had been taken, there was the lengthy task of sorting through hundreds of slides, scrutinizing them on the light box and making often very difficult decisions about which to use.

Many miles and rolls of film later, the deadline loomed and it was time to make the final choices and hand the pictures over. Despite the difficulties, I have learnt an awful lot about this wonderful area and feel privileged to have been asked to record it as best I could in the time given. I hope that this book provides some inspiration to encourage you to explore further the streets and hidden corners, and join in the customs and events, of these wonderful villages. Do it soon if you can, before there are too many changes.

PHOTOGRAPHIC EQUIPMENT

The cameras used were: Nikon 35mm SLR (F90 and F90X) with various lenses ranging from wide angle 18mm up to telephoto 300mm, and Mamiya 645 medium format with 35mm and 80mm lenses. Films used were mainly Fuji Velvia 50ASA for its fine grain, some Fuji Provia 100F, Sensia 200 and Kodak 100VS. For the Castleton Garland Ceremony, Provia 100F was pushed to 200ASA, as lighting was low. A sturdy Manfrotto tripod was used on most occasions, particularly when using slow film such as Velvia. A limited use was made of filters, namely: a polariser to cut out reflections, enhance cloud formations and saturate colours, and a grey graduate filter to even out large tonal differences in an image, usually between bright sky and dark foreground, which the eye can cope with but film cannot.

Villages in History

There are really two Peak Districts – the rugged and forbidding gritstone moorlands of the Dark Peak, and the sweet, pastoral meadows and dales of the limestone White Peak. This great geological divide has had a profound and lasting effect on the impact that man has made on the landscape, and nowhere is this more vividly shown than in the villages of the Peak District.

The buildings which make up the villages of the Peak are almost always built of the abundant native stone, and in these settlements, a distinctive vernacular architecture has developed which closely reflects the underlying geology.

So in the limestone area of the White Peak, cottages are mostly built of limestone rubble, usually with more regular gritstone quoins and window surrounds. On the outskirts of almost every village, a small scar in the hillside, usually pretty well healed by nature now, reveals the local quarry from where the stone for the buildings was excavated. No wonder that the villages seem to grow almost organically from the surrounding countryside, for it was from there that they had their Genesis.

In the warm-brown gritstone houses of the larger White Peak villages such as Bakewell, the older houses were orginally thatched by heather or roofed with thin gritstone slabs, which have often today been replaced by blue Welsh slates.

In sharp contrast, in the smaller, more isolated villages of the Dark Peak, every building is constructed from the easily available brown to clerical-grey outcrops of millstone grit, usually taken from the surrounding moors. Taking shelter in the lee of the bleak moorland, typical Dark Peak villages such as Edale, Hathersage and Baslow are almost always valley settlements, whose economy was traditionally based on hill, particularly sheep, farming.

Out in the countryside too, the barns and farm buildings also reflect the available building stone, and the theme is repeated in the endless miles of drystone walls of the Peak District – a feature which often leaves the most lasting impression to visitors, especially those coming from the South. In some walls which cross the geological divide, the type of stone can change in the length of one field wall, as the bedrock changes beneath.

Hathersage church lies beneath the gritstone mass of Higger Tor.

5

Crinoid (sea lily) and shell fossils in a limestone wall.

THE ROCKS BENEATH

As stated above, two quite distinct regions have shaped both the landscape and the buildings of Peak District villages. They are the central limestone plateau of the White Peak, between Ashbourne and Castleton, and the high millstone grit moorlands in the east, west and north of the region, which are known generically as the Dark Peak. The majority of the rocks of the area were laid down in semi-tropical conditions during the Carboniferous age, around 280–345 million years ago, when what was to become the Peak District was several degrees south of the equator and flooded by a warm, shallow sea. The enormously-thick beds of limestone which are now exposed as the White Peak plateau were laid down as countless millions of tiny sea creatures died and drifted down to the sea bed.

Following a series of minor volcanic interludes, the limestone was covered by beds of coarse grit and silt laid down by rivers flowing from the north. This was compressed and compacted to form the alternating layers of millstone grit and softer shales which now form the moorland areas known as the Dark Peak and the broad shale valleys below, now occupied by the Peak District's major rivers such as the Derwent and Wye.

At the end of the Carboniferous period, these sedimentary rocks were subjected to enormously strong folding and faulting, followed by an uplift in the earth's crust which created the famous Derbyshire Dome and, incidentally, the rest of the Pennine anticline.

Gradual erosion and denudation, accelerated by the action of glaciers and the frost-thaw conditions of successive Ice Ages wore down the dome from the centre, creating the now-familiar up-turned horseshoe of gritstone and shale with the coal measures on either side, and the older limestone exposed in the middle. It is most easily compared to the balding pate of a man's head, the White Peak limestone forming the exposed scalp at the centre, with the shales, grits and coal measures representing the remaining 'hair' on either side and at the back.

HUMAN HISTORY

As the last glaciers of the Ice Age retreated around twelve thousand years ago, they left a Peak District landscape much like the tundra of northern Canada or Greenland of today. Trees such as pine, birch, lime and ash, quickly colonised the bleak landscape and thick forests soon cloaked the dale bottoms, spreading up to cover even the highest moorlands of Kinder Scout and Bleaklow. Evidence of this extensive forest cover can still be seen in the weathered birch boles which can be seen emerging from the sides of the thick peat groughs of these now-barren moors.

And it is here, in what are now perhaps the most inhospitable places in the area, that some of the first evidence of man's presence in the Peak can still be found by the observant visitor. Tiny slivers of flint – known to archaeologists as microliths – can sometimes be picked up from the sides of those groughs or hags. These miniscule fragments of imported stone were hafted onto arrows which were discarded or lost by Mesolithic (Middle Stone Age) hunters perhaps as much as ten thousand years ago.

Few remains of the temporary camp sites of these first hunter-gatherers have survived, but in the caves and rock shelters in the sides of the White Peak dales, flint knives and scrapers have been found which date from the time of the last Ice Age.

Many of the great prehistoric monuments of the Peak District are found in the White Peak, where pastoral farming practices have served to preserve them. Principal among these is the isolated prostrate stone circle and henge monument at Arbor Low, high on the White Peak plateau near Youlgreave, which is sometimes dubbed 'the Stonehenge of the North', and dates from the same period as its much better-known Wiltshire counterpart.

Arbor Low – 'the Stonehenge of the North'.

Most remains from the prehistoric peroid show us not how these first permanent settlers lived, but how they died. The Neolithic, or New Stone Age, chambered tombs of Minninglow, near Aldwark, and Five Wells above Taddington, show how the more important members of society were buried in stone cists – from where their bones may have been periodically removed for certain ceremonial or ritual occasions.

Moving into the Bronze Age, it is again the evidence of burial practices which tell us most in the modern landscape about how these people lived. There are estimated to be at least 500 barrows or burial mounds – scattered across the White Peak dating from this period. Nearly all are situated on hilltops or high points in the landscape, and paradoxically most have the suffix 'low' from the Old English 'hlaw' indicating a burial mound or hill.

It is in this period, dating from perhaps 2700 years ago, that the first real evidence of farming and settlement can be traced, mainly

on the eastern moors of the Peak District. Here, on places like Big Moor and Gardom's Edge, systematic archaeological investigation has led to clearance cairns, field systems, hut circles and burial mounds being identified. It seems that arable fields grew crops and sizeable communities lived and thrived on these now bleak moorlands.

The Iron Age (about two thousand years ago) was the age of the hillfort, and impressive examples can be found at places like Mam Tor at the head of the Hope Valley and Fin Cop, overlooking Monsal Dale. These huge banked and ditched enclosures were once thought to be purely military in origin, but are now believed to have more peaceful uses, perhaps as summer sheilings from where the tribes' livestock could be observed. But again, very little remains, except for isolated random finds, to show us how these people – part of a large North Country tribe known as the Brigantians – lived.

It was the abundant and easily accessible lead ore found in the limestone areas of the White Peak which first attracted the Romans into Derbyshire, in the latter part of the first century. Forts were built at Navio, near Brough in the Hope Valley, and at Melandra, near Glossop at the entrance to Longdendale. Later, a more substantial settlement was made around the warm springs at Buxton (Aquae Arnemetiae), and a Roman milestone was found in the grounds of Haddon Hall.

The great mystery of the four centuries of Roman occupation of the Peak District is the whereabouts of the lead mining centre known as Lutudarum, whose name has been found moulded into several pigs of Roman lead which were exported all over Britain, but which has still to be conclusively identified.

The Roman period was a largely settled one in the Peak District, as in the rest of the country. Many small Romano-British farms and even villas sprung up in the county, some of which, such as the sites at Roystone Grange, near Ballidon and Chee Tor, near Blackwell, have been excavated.

We now also know that the period between the Romans and the Normans – usually termed in history books as the Dark Ages – was anything but dark. It saw a wonderful flowering of art and sculpture which is witnessed by the Peak's outstanding collection of Dark Age

Saxon preaching crosses – the finest outside Northumbria. Excellent examples can be found at Bakewell, Eyam, Hope and Ilam.

The first Anglian people who colonised the Peak District were known as the Pecsaetan, or people of the hill country. For a period, the Peak District appears to have acted as a buffer between the states of Mercia and Northumbria before Mercia finally attained ascendancy by the end of the eighth century.

By this time, the Saxon kingdom of Wessex held sway over the whole of Derbyshire under the rule of King Edward the Elder, the eldest son of Alfred the Great. According to the *Anglo-Saxon Chronicle*, Edward travelled north in 920 to Bakewell, where he built a fortress (a burh) in the neighbourhood.

Many of the preaching crosses date from this period, when Christianity first arrived in the area, and it is thought that the large number of carved stones found in Bakewell church may mean that it was the site of a flourishing school of Mercian sculpture at this time.

By the time of the Norman Conquest, much of the present-day pattern of villages and towns in the Peak was well-established, as is illustrated by the *Domesday Book* of 1086. Bakewell is one of only seven churches in Derbyshire which are mentioned as having a priest and being in existence before the Conquest, but only Bakewell and Ilam still show signs of Saxon work today.

Much of what we now know as the Peak District was held by the king at the time of Domesday, as part of the Royal Forest of the Peak – a 40-square-mile hunting ground preserved for royalty. The forest was administered as were the king's lead mines, from Peveril Castle at Castleton, built by William Peverel, one of the Conquerer's illegitimate sons, who also built the original stronghold at Haddon Hall, near Bakewell.

Peveril Castle, high on its almost impregnable crag between the Peak Cavern Gorge and Cave Dale, is one of the earliest stone-built keeps in the country. Built around 1170, the keep was added by Henry II, who was a frequent visitor to the Forest. The earliest part of the castle is the curtain wall along the northern side of the castle crag. The planned township of Castleton, which never quite filled the area contained by its town ditch beneath the castle walls, was probably also the work of Henry.

A frosty winter view of Haddon Hall, near Bakewell.

Even earlier than this were the so-called motte-and-bailey castles of the earliest years of Norman rule. Examples of these can be seen at Pilsbury, in the Upper Dove Valley and at Bakewell, standing guard over the town bridge. During the Middle Ages, the wealth of the Peak District was founded on its lead and wool, and some of the fine churches, such as the beautiful, Perpendicular-towered 'Cathedral of the Peak' at Tideswell, and All Saints at Youlgreave are founded on those riches.

The Middle Ages also saw the growth of the large estates, and the great Derbyshire families such as the Cavendishes, Dukes of Devonshire, at Chatsworth and the Vernons at Haddon, grew rich on them and their produce, building the region's matchless heritage of stately homes and parklands.

This was also the time of the first enclosures of the large medieval open fields from the moorland which still covered much of the upland part of the county. These large, irregular fields on the outskirts of villages contrast strongly with the narrow linear fields leading from the village crofts which were the villager's own strip fields.

The pattern of medieval enclosure is well shown in White Peak villages such as Chelmorton, Monyash and Wardlow, where it has been 'fossilised' by the drystone walls. At other places, such as around Tissington, the corrugated ridge-and-furrow patterns created by medieval oxen ploughing teams still stand out, especially in low light or light snow. On steeper slopes, cultivation terraces known as lynchets, still visible, show that every available piece of land had to be used to grow crops in times of hardship.

But there are many more seemingly inexplicable bumps and hollows which show up in Peak District meadows. These can consist of square-cut platforms and depressions, and the hollows and hillocks which spread in straight, diagonal lines across many limestone pastures. The first category show the area's legacy of deserted medieval villages (DMVs), examples of which can be found at Nether Haddon, opposite Haddon Hall, Conksbury, Smerril and Ballidon.

The cause of the depopulation is usually not simply the Black Death, as is often claimed. There were many reasons for such large-scale abandonment, including most commonly the desire of the landowner to introduce more profitable sheep grazing or cropping; his need to improve the view from his great house; the failure of a site for geographical reasons, and disease or pestilence.

The linear bumps and hollows on the limestone plateau are evidence of the work of 't'owd man' – the local name for former lead miners. Lead mining was an important industry in the White Peak for well over one thousand years, starting with the Romans and ending in the 1870s, when cheaper imports became available. There are estimated to be about 30,000 abandoned workings in the area, the best preserved of which is the Magpie Mine, near Sheldon, which was worked more or less continuously for two hundred years. It is now used as a field-study centre by the Peak District Mines Historical Society.

Peak District lead miners were usually farmers as well, and this dual economy existed in the area as the mainstay of the local economy for centuries, bequeathing a rich legacy in the language and landscape. One of the greatest problems facing the lead miner was water flooding the lower reaches of the mines, and enormous sums were spent on 'de-watering' mines by underground drainage channels known as soughs.

Ironically, it was the power of the Derbyshire rivers – particularly the Derwent – which attracted the first real industrialists to the county.

Foremost among these was Richard Arkwright, who built the first successful water-powered cotton mill at Cromford in 1771, the first model village for his workers nearby, and other cotton mills at Cressbrook, Bakewell and elsewhere.

Cressbrook Mill

All this industrialisation proved the need for better communications, and the Peak District can also lay claim to being the birthplace of the founder of the canal system. James Brindley, a largely illiterate millwright was born at Tunstead, near Buxton, in 1716. A brilliant, self-taught civil engineer, he went on to build the world's first canal for the Duke of Bridgewater in 1759, as well as the Trent and Mersey or Grand Trunk Canal and the Oxford Canal, among many others.

The Cromford Canal was built by William Jessop, but it was his son who heralded the coming of the Railway Age by the design and construction of the Cromford and High Peak Railway running 33 miles across the 1000-foot White Peak plateau in 1830. First designed as a canal or waggonway (the stations were called wharfs), it was to link the Cromford Canal with the High Peak Canal at Whaley Bridge by the ingenious use of steam-operated continuous chain inclines.

The massive limestone Plum Buttress in Cheedale, with the line of the former Midland Railway on the left.

Other railways followed, and the Midland Railway established its locomotive and carriage works at Derby soon after its formation. The construction of the Midland Line, providing the lucrative link between London and Manchester through the Wye Valley and the hills of the Peak District, in 1863, attracted the wrath of early conservationists like John Ruskin. It was an amazing feat of Victorian civil engineering, and is now followed by the Monsal Trail, although there are long-term plans for its eventual reopening for passenger traffic.

Other important railways which opened up the hills and dales of the Peak were the Great Central Line from Sheffield to Glossop through

the infamous Woodhead tunnels and Longdendale, built in 1847 and now the Longdendale Trail; and the Hope Valley line, built in 1894 to link Sheffield and Stockport through Edale and still open mainly as a 'ramblers' route'.

CUSTOMS AND TRADITIONS

The isolation of Peak District villages is often cited as the reason for the survival of an unusually large number of traditional customs, the best-known of which is well dressing. This unique form of folk art was originally confined to the limestone villages of the White Peak, but has now spread all over the Peak District and well beyond, to more than 50 villages.

No one really knows how and when the tradition started, although the most widely accepted explanation is that it originated as a pagan oblation to the gods who provided the life-giving gift of water on the fast-draining limestone plateau.

The first recorded example of village wells being dressed by flowers and other natural decoration was at Tissington during the terrible years of the Black Death in 1348–49, when the purity of the water was said to have perserved the villagers from the dread disease. The tradition was revived during a prolonged drought in the same village in 1615, when miraculously the wells kept flowing. Tissington is still the earliest well dressing in the Peak District calendar, timed to coincide with Ascension Day each year.

Most other villages time their well dressings for the local Wakes Weeks, when the patron saint of the parish church is remembered, and when there was once a public holiday. Today's well dressings almost always have a Christian, biblical theme, although national or local anniversaries are sometimes celebrated.

For a detailed step-by-step pictorial account of the construction of a typical well dressing, see 'The Art of Well Dressing' on pages 12–15.

Another custom which survives and prospers in the Peak is the Castleton Garlanding, a strange ceremony held every Oak Apple Day (May 29) in the Hope Valley village of Castleton. Again, this is thought to have pagan origins, and consists of a procession which passes through the village, calling at every public house en route, to finish up at the parish church of St Edmund beneath the castle walls.

Leading the procession on horseback is the 'King' – a man dressed in Stuart costume – whose head and shoulders are completely covered in a huge bell-shaped wooden cone which is decorated with flowers and leaves. He is accompanied by his 'Queen' and a troup of white-dressed local children who dance to a tune which is very similar to the Cornish Floral Dance. When the procession reaches the church, the garland is hoisted off the King's shoulders to the top of the church church, where it is left to wither and die.

The Eyam Plague Commemoration held on the last Sunday of August commemorates and gives thanks for the villagers who died after imposing a voluntary quarantine when the plague struck there in 1665–6. A service is held at Cucklett Delph, where services were held during the terrible 'visitation' is which 259 people died in their brave attempt to stop the infection from spreading.

Other customs include a thriving Morris dancing tradition which is particularly strong in Winster with its own team and tunes, and Bakewell's famous culinary speciality, the Bakewell pudding (never, incidentally, known as a 'tart' here). At least three local shops claim to have the original recipe, which was created as a result of a mistake by a cook at the inn where the Rutland Arms now stands.

Bakewell's agricultural market, now held in the new Agricultural and Business Centre, still brings together the farming community of the Peakland villages every Monday, as it has for centuries, and another weekly farmers' market is held at Hope. Also based on the predom-inant sheep-farming industry are the annual sheepdog trials, such as those held at Dovedale, Longshaw and Bamford.

THE NATIONAL PARK

The Peak District National Park was the first to be designated in Britain in 1951, in recognition of the need to protect this island of out-standing and largely unspoilt scenery hemmed in by some of the largest industrial cities of northern England, particulary Sheffield and Manchester. It covers a total of 555 square miles between Ashbourne in the south and Holme in the north. One of the most important jobs

with which the National Park Authority is charged is to control harmful and unsuitable development within its area. This has meant that the unique and unspoilt character of the Peak's villages has largely been maintained.

This has been achieved despite the fact that the social dynamics of many villages have changed dramatically in recent years. As house prices have soared, young local people find it increasingly difficult to buy their own homes in Peak District villages, allowing wealthier incomers to move in. As these are often older, retired people, the numbers on the roll of the village school start to fall, and it may close, signalling the end of a vibrant, young village community. Village shops and post offices too, are under threat, as a more mobile population prefers to go into the nearest town supermarket for the bulk of its shopping.

Over 22 million day-visits are made to the National Park every year, making it the second-most visited National Park in the world. Those visitors who flock to the scenic hills and dales of the Peak often find themselves equally attracted to the rich heritage of charming towns and villages, each with its own sharply defined character, architecture and traditions.

Thorpe Cloud and the Stepping Stones at the entrance to Dovedale.

The Art of Well Dressing

Well dressing in the Peak District is a unique example of folk art which involves the whole village community and attracts thousands of admirers every year. It takes the form of an intricately-constructed floral icon in which, in its purest form, only natural materials such as flower petals and seeds which can be collected locally, are used.

The following is a ten-part, step-by-step account of a typical well dressing, using the examples of the villages of Tideswell and Little Longstone.

1   DESIGN

Paul Fletcher hard at work on the initial designs for a Tideswell well dressing. The design is taken from a photograph which is first photocopied and enlarged, traced onto plain paper with a grid, and then enlarged again and traced onto plain newsprint for eventual 'pricking out' onto the clay.

2   COLLECTING

Villagers scour the surrounding countryside for seeds, flowers, lichens and other natural materials for the dressing. It is not unknown for cottage gardens to be secretly 'raided' at this time!

3   SOAKING THE BOARDS

The wooden boards which will frame the dressing have to be soaked for several days in the local river or stream to ensure they retain moisture. Here the Little Longstone dressers are collecting their boards after a week's soaking in the River Wye.

4 PUDDLING THE CLAY

This is the mucky bit that the children love. Youngsters from Little Longstone 'puddling' the wet clay with their wellington-booted feet to make it pliable and sticky, ready to take the petals. Salt is sometimes added to inhibit the clay from drying out.

5 PUTTING THE CLAY IN THE BOARDS

The clay is then pressed firmly into place in the boards and smoothed over to create a good, even surface to take the dressing.

6 PRICKING OUT

Now the paper template of the design is 'picked out' onto the wet clay, using a pin wheel or other sharp instrument.

7 'BLACK KNOBBING'

The next stage is to outline the design in the clay using black alder cones, seeds or wool, so that petalling can start.

8 PETALLING

This is the real art of a well dressing, as villagers carefully press down flower petals, mosses, lichens, grass and rushes to colour in and shade the design. The petals are pressed down so that they overlap like roof tiles, thus ensuring some degree of water-shedding if it rains.

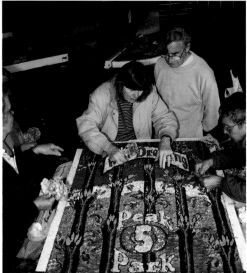

9 ERECTION OF THE BOARDS

Finally, the boards are erected near the village well, spring or pump, roped off and decorated to stand for about a week and be admired by thousands of visitors. This was Little Longstone's dressing which marked the fiftieth anniversary of the Peak District National Park in 2001.

10 THE FINISHED PRODUCT

A close-up (opposite) of the finished product of one of Tideswell's 1998 well dressings, which shows in detail the fine mosaic petalling skills of the well-dressers. The picture shows the parish church of St Mary on the other River Wye at Ross in Herefordshire.

The Villages and Map

For the purposes of this book, the Peak District has been split into four geographical areas. They are:

1. THE SOUTHERN WHITE PEAK
From the valley of the Wye south to Dovedale

2. THE CENTRAL WHITE PEAK
From the Wye north to Castleton

3. THE NORTHERN AND EASTERN DARK PEAK
The valley of the Derwent and the moors to the north of Castleton

4. THE WESTERN DARK PEAK
West of the Dove

SOUTHERN WHITE PEAK

The White Peak to the south of the River Wye and Bakewell is an uplifted plateau
of pearly-grey limestone which is dissected by steep-sided dales. Villages like Youlgreave,
Hartington and Monyash sit in shallow, slightly sheltered bowls on the exposed
limestone plateau. The most spectacular and best known of the dales are those
formed by the Dove, Lathkill, Bradford and Manifold.

Alport *An idyllic, ivy-clad cottage by the side of the River Bradford at Alport – a popular candidate for the prettiest village in the Peak District. Standing at the junction of the Rivers Bradford and Lathkill, Alport contains many fine sixteenth- and seventeenth-century farms and cottages.*

Alsop-en-le-Dale *Alsop's parish church of St Michael sits at the centre of this general view of the village, which is tucked onto the side of a dry dale just off the A515 north of Ashbourne. The church was originally Norman, but what we see today is largely a Victorian reconstruction.*

Alsop-en-le-Dale *Alsop Hall is a tall and distinguished pre-classical seventeenth-century building, featuring mullioned windows and stately gables on its symmetrical façade. But Nikolaus Pevsner's rather scathing comment on the building in his* Buildings of England – Derbyshire *(1953) was that it was 'much renewed'.*

Alstonefield *A rambling party, probably headed for Dovedale, gathers outside The George public house on the green in the centre of Alstonefield. The George is a well-known walkers' pub, ideally situated in this quiet Staffordshire village which stands on the limestone plateau to the west of the enticing upper reaches of Dovedale.*

Bonsall *Carnival buntings converge on the ball-topped cross which stands in the centre of the sloping market place in the former lead mining village of Bonsall. The seventeenth-century cross stands on a distinctive plinth of natural gritstone featuring 13 concentric steps – a natural focal point for the villagers.*

Bonsall *This forlorn field barn, seen through a veil of cow parsley near the village of Bonsall, tells the sad story of many such buildings, which are such important features of the White Peak landscape. No longer required by farmers for keeping winter hay, they quickly fall into disrepair, and once the roof has gone as in this case, the end of these characteristic buildings is not far away.*

Brassington *Springtime arrives in the hillside village of Brassington, with the solid tower of the Norman parish church of St James dominating the middle distance. Brassington is in the heart of lead-mining country, and there is much evidence of 't'owd man' – the old lead miners – in the surrounding fields.*

Brassington *A veteran car passes a splendid gabled Tudor house, dated 1615, in the centre of Brassington. The mullioned and transomed windows tell of a wealthy owner, who perhaps gained his wealth from the abundant lead mines which once surrounded the village.*

Chelmorton *A tractor holds up the traffic (one car!) in Church Lane, Chelmorton, high on the White Peak plateau. Chelmorton, standing at well over 1000 feet, is one of the highest villages in England, and is renowned for its surviving medieval strip fields, now 'fossilised' by drystone walls, seen running away towards the main village street to the right of this photograph.*

Chelmorton *Another view of Chelmorton – or 'Chelly' as it affectionately known – showing the lower slopes of Chelmorton Low in the background and the elegant, fifteenth-century spire of the parish church of St John the Baptist on the right. Two Bronze-Age burial mounds top the 1463ft-summit of Chelmorton Low, evidence of the continuity of occupation on the high White Peak plateau.*

Earl Sterndale *A fine Friesian cow eyes the photographer quizzically in this unusual view of Earl Sterndale, in the limestone hills to the south of Buxton. In the background, illuminated by a stormy sun, is the tower of the nineteenth-century parish church of St Michael, and the distinctive profiles of Chrome and Parkhouse Hills.*

Hartington *Flower-filled fields and an intricate pattern of drystone walls encompass the pretty White Peak village of Hartington, seen here from one of the many footpaths which lead out from its centre. The solid, hilltop parish church of St Giles, seen here in the distance on the right, is one of the most interesting in the Peak, with a unique two-storey porch and massive Perpendicular tower watching over the village as it has for over five hundred years.*

Hartington *The classical, three-arched arcade of Hartington's town hall was built in 1836 and adds an air of urban dignity to the village square, which is surrounded by elegant eighteenth- and nineteenth-century town houses, like those seen on the right of this photograph.*

Hartington *Tudor-built Hartington Hall Youth Hostel, just outside the village centre, boasts one of the most distinguished 'overnights' of any youth hostel in Britain. Bonnie Prince Charlie is alleged to have stayed here in 1745 on his ill-fated march on London, and the room where he is supposed to have slept is still pointed out to visitors to this recently-refurbished and quite palatial hostel.*

Ilam *A glorious early autumnal view south-east towards Ilam, taken from the slopes of Buntser Hill, which guards the entrance to Dovedale. The trees on the extreme left horizon are Hazelton Clump and the pond in the foreground is at Home Farm.*

Ilam *The Gothic Eleanor-type village cross in the centre of the pretty estate village of Ilam, on the Staffordshire bank of the River Dove, is a memorial to Mary, the wife of Jesse Watts-Russell, a Victorian shipping magnate who redesigned the village in the* cottage ornée *style we see today.*

Ilam *The Dovedale Sheepdog trials held near Ilam every August attract competitors from all over the country. Here, a competitor's collie dog waits, paw raised, to be called into action. Some of the best sheepdog handlers in Britain hail from the villages of the Peak District.*

Middleton-by-Youlgreave *Two walkers enjoy a well-earned rest in the village square of Middleton-by-Youlgreave, a prosperous settlement just to the south of its larger neighbour, above the leafy ravine of Bradford Dale. Middleton is perhaps best known as the former home of the Peak's most distinguished Victorian antiquary and archaeologist, Thomas Bateman.*

Milldale *'Why a mouse can hardly go over it: 'Tis not two fingers broad.' That was Viator's response in Izaak Walton's* The Compleat Angler *to his first sight of this tiny packhorse bridge which crosses the River Dove near the pretty hamlet of Milldale. Nowadays, the only traffic are walkers on the well-worn path which runs through perhaps the Peak's most famous dale, Dovedale.*

Monyash *The seventeenth-century Bull's Head at Monyash has now thankfully had its ancient name restored, after an unfortunate period when it was misguidedly renamed The Hobbit. Monyash is another former lead-mining village, which was awarded its market charter as long ago as 1340. The ancient village cross, seen here in the fore-ground, has watched over the village green since those medieval times.*

Monyash *Reflected in the still waters of Fere Mere, one of several ponds which were used to water the stock on the fast-draining limestone plateau, the spire of the parish church of St Leonard dominates in this winter view of Monyash.*

Over Haddon *The hilltop position of Over Haddon above the crystal waters of Lathkill Dale is well illustrated in this photograph, taken from the footpath which leads up from Conksbury Bridge. The weirs in the Lathkill, seen here on the left, were constructed to encourage the breeding of trout in this famous fishing river.*

Over Haddon *The village pump at Over Haddon. Water supplies were vitally important on the fast-draining limestone plateau of the White Peak, so the pump, wells or springs were venerated in ancient, pagan times, which many people think gave rise to the modern custom of well dressing.*

Over Haddon *No one can date this ancient clapper bridge over the River Lathkill below Over Haddon, but we know it has been there linking the village with monastic Meadow Place Grange on the hilltop opposite for many centuries. The only thing to spoil the picture is the unnecessary handrail, which disfigures this ancient monument.*

Parwich *The village pond – locally known as a 'mere' – in the pretty White Peak village of Parwich was once used to wash sheep before shearing. Today it forms the centrepiece of the village, where limestone cottages with well-kept gardens cluster around in tasteful order.*

Sheldon *A couple of inquisitive steers watch the camera suspiciously in front of a traditional limestone longhouse in Sheldon. Note the limestone-rubble walls and gritstone tiles, and the windows to the right which once were living quarters.*

Sheldon *Despite its ancient appearance, the Cock and Pullet public house at Sheldon is one of the Peak's newest pubs. It was converted from it former use as a barn in 1995, and is famous for its wonderful collection of chiming clocks. The former village pub was the Devonshire Arms which stood next door but closed in 1971.*

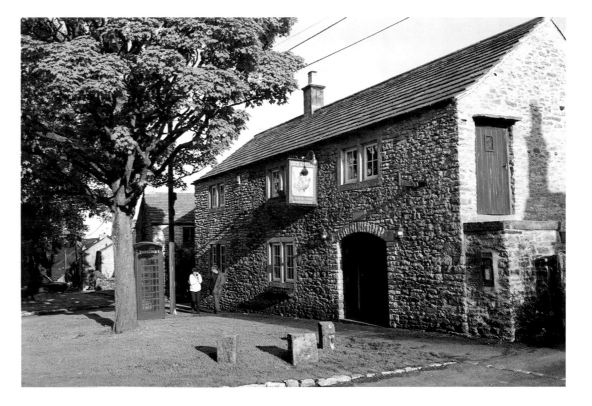

Stanton-in-the-Peak *Colourful tulips and flowering shrubs adorn this gritstone cottage doorway in the hillside village of Stanton-in-the-Peak, near Bakewell. The carvings over the door show that it was built in 1900, and that it is part of the Thornhill estate, along with most of the cottages in the village.*

Stanton–in–the–Peak *Stanton lies on the edge of Stanton Moor, a gritstone inlier in limestone country which has been quarried for its building stone for centuries. Some of these quarries now threaten some of the rich prehistoric remains on the moor, and this shot of Stanton Post Office shows one of the committed group of protesters who are encamped on the moor in an effort to stop further quarrying.*

Tissington *Springtime in the White Peak village of Tissington is a magical time, when fields of daffodils burst into bloom by the village mere, and the village prepares for its well dressing, traditionally the first of the season.*

Tissington *The village's famous well dressings are generally regarded as the earliest to be recorded, and they attract thousands of visitors every year. This picture shows the Coffin Well display in 2002, which followed a traditonal biblical theme.*

Tissington *The start of well dressing week in Tissington, which usually coincides with Ascension Day, is marked by the blessing of the wells by local priests, who in 2002 included the Bishop in his mitre.*

Tissington *Jacobean Tissington Hall dominates the village, and has been the home of the FitzHerbert family, whose estate covers 2400 acres of the village and surrounding countryside, for five hundred years. The Hall and gardens were recently reopened to the public by the present occupant, Sir Richard FitzHerbert.*

Tissington *Farmer Hazel Bailey, from Wibbern Hill Farm, Tissington, cheerfully feeds her chickens and new-born lambs. It is a timeless scene, which could have been enacted in a Peakland farmyard at any time in the last five hundred years.*

Winster *Winster Hall, seen here on a bright spring morning, is a classical eighteeenth-century Palladian house which fronts the village's main street. It was once the home of Llewellyn Jewitt, the distinguished late-nineteenth-century antiquary and illustrator. Note the pedimented doorway and balustrades around the top of the three-storey façade.*

Winster *A customer inspects the flowers for sale outside Winster's General Stores, an important focus of this beautifully-complete, mainly eighteenth-century village. Winster's wealth was founded, like so many White Peak villages, on lead mining and farming.*

Winster *The Old Market House in the centre of Winster was the first property to be acquired by the National Trust in the Peak District in 1906. It dates from the end of the seventeenth century, and originally had an open, arched ground floor, much like that of nearby Bakewell, where trading took place.*

Winster *This charming garden leads to the arched doorway of Winster's former Parish Poorhouse, which lies on the edge of the village near the Miners' Standard public house. This was where the poor of the village lived when they were homeless, existing on the charity of their fellow villagers.*

Youlgreave *The centre of the busy village of Youlgreave above Bradford Dale, south of Bakewell, is dominated by the large circular water tank of the village's own private water supply. Known as The Fountain, it was built in 1829 and still supplies the village with its drinking water. The white-walled cottage in the centre background is the one-up, one-down Thimble Hall, thought to be the smallest house in the Peak District.*

Youlgreave *Youlgreave's Old Hall, seen here, dates from 1650 and is one of the village's finest buildings. The 'somewhat projecting symmetrical wings with five- and six-light mullioned windows and gables' were commented on by Pevsner in 1953.*

Youlgreave *A distant view, on a windy day, of the village which stands on a shelf of limestone above Bradford Dale. Prominent in the picture is the tall Perpendicular tower of the parish church of All Saints, one of the finest in the Peak.*

Youlgreave *A tumbling weir, constructed to encourage fish to breed, in the River Bradford below Youlgreave. There is a pleasant walk on the broad track seen on the right along the banks of the river, to Middleton in one direction, and Alport in the other.*

Youlgreave *The white walls of the Meadow Cottage Tea Rooms, on the lane which leads down to the footbridge which crosses the River Bradford below Youlgreave, are a welcome sight to many thirsty ramblers out walking to and from the village. Note the family (left) enjoying a spot of paddling in the river.*

CENTRAL WHITE PEAK

The central part of the White Peak, between the River Wye and its northern edge at
Castleton, has some of the biggest and oldest settlements in the Peak District, including
Bakewell, Tideswell and Castleton. The raised plateau, heavily exploited by industry
in the form of quarrying and fluorspar extraction, slopes up towards the north,
reaching its highest point near Peak Forest.

Abney *Cock of the roost. A proud cockerel, master of all he surveys, greets the photographer in an Abney garden.*

Abney *The setting of the village of Abney, tucked into a shallow depression in what was once moorland above the River Derwent, is well shown in this long-range photograph taken from Abney Moor. The outlying farm on the right is Abney Grange, which has medieval monastic connections.*

Ashford-in-the-Water *An unusual view of Ashford-in-the-Water's most-photographed feature, the medieval Sheepwash Bridge over the River Wye. Here, in the time-honoured way, sheep are still unceremoniously tossed into the river from a small enclosure by the bridge, to clean their fleeces before shearing in the summer.*

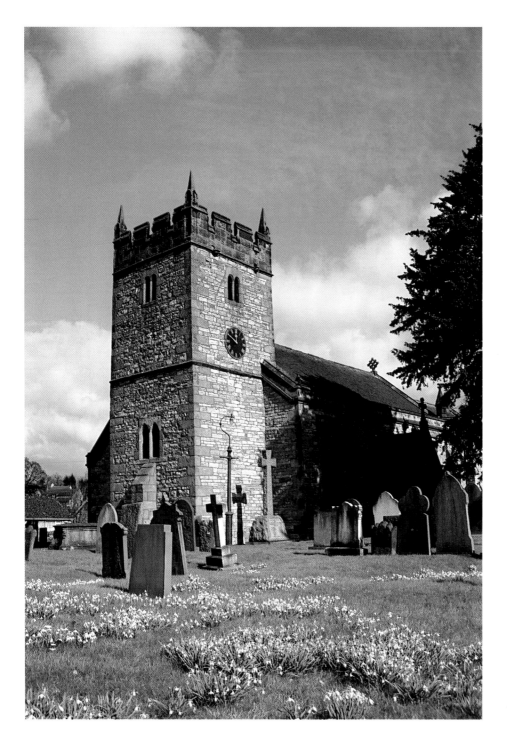

Ashford-in-the-Water *Drifts of snowdrops decorate the churchyard in this winter view of Ashford's parish church of the Holy Trinity. The solidly-built tower retains its thirteenth-century base, but the rest of the church was largely rebuilt in 1870. The interior is famed for its Ashford Black Marble (a polished local limestone) and virgin's crants (paper garlands carried at the funerals of unmarried village girls).*

Ashford-in-the-Water *The village shop at Ashford-in-the-Water is patriotically decked out for the Queen's Golden Jubilee in 2002. The village shop is usually the hub of most village activity, including the latest gossip, and its closure can mean the death knell for the community.*

Bakewell *Garlands of cherry blossom decorate this springtime view of Bakewell's medieval Town Bridge, which has carried traffic over the River Wye for over six centuries. The downstream side of the bridge, shown here, was widened but the upstream side still dates from the fourteenth century – making it one of the oldest road bridges still in use in the country.*

Bakewell *With a population of 4000, Bakewell is the largest village in the Peak District and the 'capital' of the area. The Monday agricultural market is a natural focus for the farming folk of the area, but recent improvements have also made Bakewell a fashionable shopping centre, as shown here in pedestrianised Portland Square.*

Bakewell *The village is probably best known to the outside world for its culinary delicacy, the Bakewell pudding. This Christmas view shows the the Old Original Pudding Shop in the centre of the village, which is one of three which claim to hold the original recipe and which now sends the puddings round the world.*

Bakewell *The judging of a Shire Horse Class at the annual Bakewell Agricultural Show, held every August on the riverside showground behind the modern Agricultural Business Centre, where the weekly farming market is now held. The Bakewell Show is probably the most important social event in the Peak District calendar, and is known as 'the little Royal Show'.*

Bakewell *The parish church of All Saints, Bakewell, stands in splendid isolation on a hill which overlooks the busy little market town. Largely reconstructed between 1841–52, it is noted for its octagonal tower and spire, seen here from the churchyard, where two Saxon preaching crosses hint at its early formation.*

Bradwell *A distant view of Bradwell – usually abbreviated to 'Bradder' in the way of Peak District villages – from the escarpment of Bradwell Edge. The settlement of Bradwell dates back at least to Roman times, and the foundations of the fortlet of Navio stood at its northern edge. Bradwell's fortune was founded, like so many other White Peak villages, on lead mining. Mam Tor dominates the background.*

Bradwell *It's Gala Day in Bradwell, and the camera catches the judging of the Rose Queen on the Beggar's Plot playing field. Bradwell's Gala Day in August coincides with the village's well dressings, when four wells are dressed, including one by the village children.*

Bradwell *Like Bakewell, Bradwell has its own unique culinary delicacy. 'Bradder' Ice Cream, produced until recently by the Bradwell family, is famous and in much demand locally. There is even a Bradwell Ice Cream shop in Sheffield's Meadowhall Shopping Centre!*

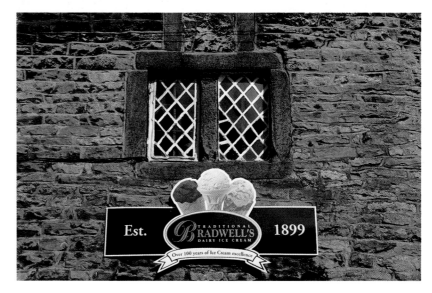

Castleton *A seasonal light dusting of snow flecks the roofs of the shops in Castleton's Cross Street at Christmas-time. 'The Castleton lights' are a popular attraction at this time of the year, as many visitors throng into the village to do some last-minute shopping, perhaps for gifts made from the local semi-precious stone speciality – Blue John.*

Castleton *The way to the impressive entrance of Peak Cavern at Castleton takes the visitor past flower-filled cottage gardens from Goose Hill Bridge along the banks of Peakshole Water, seen here on the right, which flows from the gaping cavern where a community of rope-makers once plied their trade.*

Castleton *The virtually-impregnable defensive position of Peveril Castle at Castleton is well seen in this view taken from the precipitous slopes of Cave Dale, which protect it from the south. The castle was begun shortly after the Norman Conquest, and the keep, seen here on its crag, was added by Henry II in the 1170s.*

Castleton *One of the strangest and oldest folk ceremonies in the Peak District takes place at Castleton on Oak Apple Day (May 29). Known as the Garlanding, it involves a procession around the village by the King (seen here in 2002) who is encased in a wooden-framed pyramid of flowers and his Queen (in the left distance), accompanied by dancers.*

Castleton *The Garland King, village postman Peter Outram, takes a crafty but well-earned pint under his garland to quench his thirst on his way around the village.*

Castleton *A smile for the camera from Rebecca, one of the dancers taking part in the Castleton Garlanding. The tune used has a strong resemblance to that of the Cornish Floral Dance, and is believed to have been brought to the village by Cornish lead miners.*

Cressbrook *Christmas time at Cressbrook Hall, a typical Victorian manor house whose outbuildings have been tastefully converted to provide high-class holiday accommodation. The Tudor-style hall was built in 1835 by the owner of the local cotton mill, and it stands in an idyllic spot, overlooking the River Wye as it flows through spectacular Miller's Dale.*

Eyam *Potted plants make a colourful show by the front door of this gritstone cottage in Eyam. Famous as the 'plague village', Eyam has many other attractions, and the villagers pride themselves on the appearance of their homes which are admired by thousands of visitors every year.*

Eyam *The parish church of St Lawrence at Eyam lay at the centre of the plague drama three centuries ago. The church dates from the thirteenth century, but the intricately-carved preaching cross in the church (centre) is much older, dating from the ninth century. Next to it is the tabletop grave of Catherine Mompesson, wife of the minister, who died during the plague.*

Eyam *Seventeenth-century Eyam Hall, seen here through the filigree of its cast iron gates, has been the home of the Wright family since it was built in 1676. Thankfully now open to the public, this fine country house retains a lovely, intimate family atmosphere, and there are some fine tapestries in the upper rooms.*

Eyam *One of the most touching memorials to the plague years is found half a mile east of the village, where these forlorn gravestones in a walled enclosure known as the Riley Graves are a vivid reminder of the effects of the dread disease. Here a mother was forced to bury her husband, three sons and three daughters all of whom died within eight days of each other in 1666.*

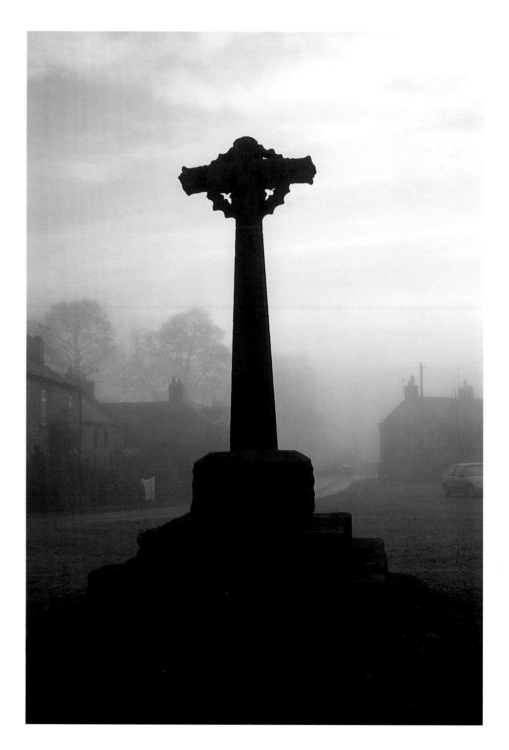

Foolow *A misty-morning shot of the medieval village cross which stands on the green at Foolow. Foolow is one of the White Peak's prettiest villages, clustered around the ancient cross, which was moved to this site on the village green in 1868 from its original site near the Wesleyan Reform Chapel.*

Foolow *A handsome white duck guards the village mere at Foolow — the focal point of the village and formerly an important source of water for stock on the relatively dry limestone plateau of the White Peak.*

Hassop *Bright spring daffodils line the grand entrance to Hassop Hall, the elegant early-seventeenth-century former home of the Eyre family, which is now a top-class restaurant and hotel. The Eyres were staunchly Roman Catholic, hence the Etruscan temple-style Catholic church which stands opposite the hall's entrance.*

Hope *A bright, blossomy spring afternoon in Hope, with the stumpy spire and tower of the fourteenth-century parish church of St Peter prominent below the shadowed lower slopes of Win Hill rising to the right. The church contains tombs of officials of the Royal Forest of the Peak, showing its former importance which gave its name to the whole valley from Hathersage to Castleton.*

Hope *The biggest employer in the Hope Valley is the cement works, seen here on a misty morning from the hills above. Although some may feel such an industrial site is wrong in a National Park, the works are here for very good reason. They are close to their raw materials of limestone and shale, they provide much-needed employment and, thankfully, most of their finished product is taken out by rail.*

Great Hucklow *Smile please! Most of the population of Great Hucklow parish, young and old, gather for an historic photograph which marked the Queen's Golden Jubilee celebrations in 2002.*

Great Hucklow *Troughs carved from gritstone front Hucklow Hall, reminders of a time when horsepower meant exactly that. Great Hucklow is a former lead-mining village under Hucklow Edge, and was once nationally-known for its outstanding amateur dramatic group led by Laurence du Garde Peach.*

Great Hucklow *The beautiful Georgian-style windows of the Old Unitarian Chapel in Great Hucklow are a reminder of the strength of Nonconformism among the local population. Originally founded in 1696, the chapel was rebuilt and moved to its present site in the late-eighteenth century, and enlarged again in 1901.*

Little Hucklow *A winter sunrise paints the vast canvas of the eastern skies in red and gold, and throws a pink reflection on the snowy fields around Little Hucklow, the home of photographer Karen Frenkel. Little Hucklow is a tiny, isolated hamlet high above the upper reaches of Bradwell Dale.*

Great Longstone *The fine, aisled parish church of St Giles at Great Longstone dates from the thirteenth century and provides a reminder of the village's important former trades. Inside are carvings of a lead miner and a milkmaid, illustrating the traditional dual economy of the White Peak – farming and mining.*

Great Longstone *The weathered market cross standing on the village green at Great Longstone dates from the time the village was first granted the right to hold a market in the Middle Ages. Today, people have to go to Bakewell for the weekly agricultural market.*

Great Longstone *The sweeping landscape of the White Peak plateau as seen from the escarpment of Longstone Edge, with the village of Great Longstone in the sunlit middle distance. Longstone Edge is riddled with lead mines, some of which are currently being re-worked for fluorspar.*

Little Longstone *A rose-covered, chocolate-box cottage in the tiny hamlet of Little Longstone. Only the modern conservatory mars the scene, as the ancient roof bows under the weight of its heavy gritstone slabs.*

Little Longstone *The tiny, towerless Victorian church at Little Longstone stands aloof from the hamlet, on the road which leads up to one of the Peak District's most famous viewpoints at Monsal Head.*

Litton *The village of Litton stands 1000 feet up on the limestone plateau, as can be seen in this view from Litton Edge. The simple one-street village runs east-west, but plainly visible are the medieval strip or burgage plots which ran out from each house, now preserved in drystone walls.*

Litton *Morris dancers are a popular attraction in summer outside the Red Lion public house in the centre of Litton. The Red Lion is a typical Peak District pub, popular now with weekend vistors and walkers.*

Litton Mill *This pretty row of terraced cottages at Litton Mill was originally built by the mill owner to house his workers. Litton Mill, now being converted to living accommodation, had an evil reputation in its early years, when owner Ellis Needham had a reputation for some of the worst examples of the exploitation of child labour in the nineteenth century.*

Peak Forest *The parish church of Peak Forest has an unusual dedication and an even more unusual history. It is one of the few churches in England dedicated to King Charles the Martyr, and this gave it extra-parochial powers which enabled couples to marry there without the banns being read. The village gets its name because it once stood at the centre of the medieval Royal Forest of the Peak.*

Peak Forest *Seen from the track which takes the walker up to Eldon Hole, the biggest open pothole in the Peak and one of the original 'Wonders of the Peak', the village of Peak Forest basks in the low light of late afternoon.*

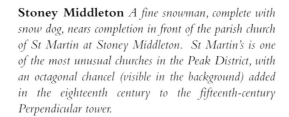

Stoney Middleton *A fine snowman, complete with snow dog, nears completion in front of the parish church of St Martin at Stoney Middleton. St Martin's is one of the most unusual churches in the Peak District, with an octagonal chancel (visible in the background) added in the eighteenth century to the fifteenth-century Perpendicular tower.*

Stoney Middleton *The centre of the busy village of Stoney Middleton, which suffers from being on the main Chesterfield to Manchester road. Note the octagonal Toll House, dated 1840 (right), which now serves as the village fish and chip shop.*

Stoney Middleton *If it were not for the busy A623 and the limestone quarries on its southern side, Stoney Middleton Dale would be one of the showplaces of the Peak. Here we see the great limestone crag known as Lover's Leap, named after a jilted local girl who leapt from it in despair, only to be saved by her voluminous skirts which acted as a parachute.*

Taddington *A fading winter sun lights the silent monoliths of the Five Wells Chambered Tomb, near Taddington. This Neolithic monument originally contained 17 skeletons and was placed in a deliberately prominent position over 1300 feet up some four thousand years ago by New Stone Age people who, seemingly, wanted their ancestors to watch over them.*

Taddington *A view across the village of Taddington, bypassed by the A6 Bakewell–Buxton road, and a typical, one-street White Peak settlement leading up to the parish church of St Michael and sheltering in the lee of Taddington Moor.*

Tideswell *The pinnacled tower of St John's dominates this view across the rooftops of Tideswell, a large village of ancient foundation which has the prosperous air of a small town. In the background is the escarpment of Hucklow Edge.*

Tideswell *A winter view of St John the Baptist parish church at Tideswell, universally known as 'the Cathedral of the Peak'. This beautiful building was built in the remarkably quick time of about seventy years from 1300, and thus is almost entirely of the then-fashionable Decorated style.*

Tideswell *A jumble of houses marches up the hill of Townend, Tideswell. Many Peak District villages, some very small, have areas known as Townend, as all were termed townships in the Middle Ages.*

Tideswell *Children dance around the maypole in Tideswell's Pot Market as part of the celebrations which marked the Queen's Golden Jubilee in 2002. The Pot Market by the parish church got its name because this was where pots and pans were sold when Tideswell held a weekly market.*

Tideswell *The village's well dressings – four are usually dressed – are held on the Saturday nearest the patronal festival of St John the Baptist's Day, 24 June. This fine example is the main Town Well which traditonally chooses a British cathedral for the subject of its main panel.*

Wardlow *A dramatic sky illuminates Peter's Stone, a strange, isolated limestone butte just outside the village of Wardlow. This was the scene of the last gibbeting in Derbyshire in 1815. Anthony Lingard was executed for the murder of Hannah Oliver from nearby Wardlow Mires.*

Wardlow *A farmer feeds his sheep on a frosty winter morning in the icy fields near Wardlow, which is seen in the middle distance. Wardlow is a typical linear, one-street village surrounded by a network of drystone walls, many of which mark medieval strip fields leading off from the village street.*

Wormhill *A carved corbel on the entrance archway to Wormhill's parish church of St Margaret shows a bearded man, perhaps someone who was known to the carver. Only the base of the west tower is medieval; the rest of the church was largely rebuilt by the Victorians in 1864.*

Wormhill *Even a bright-red telephone box can offer some kind of shelter in a typical winter blizzard at Wormhill, high on the White Peak plateau just to the east of Buxton. Wormhill stands high above Chee Dale, with Monks Dale, part of the Derbyshire Dales National Nature Reserve, to the east.*

Wormhill *Wormhill Hall, seen here through a tracery of winter trees and with a foreground dusted with snowdrops, is a late-seventeenth century, H-shaped manor house, typical of its type in the Peak District. The date of 1697 is recorded on a gutterhead on the building.*

NORTHERN AND EASTERN DARK PEAK

Grim gritstone 'edges' frown down onto the verdant shale valley of the River Derwent
on the eastern side of the Peak District, with rough moorland beyond. In these fertile
valleys the houses of large landowners, such as the Devonshires of Chatsworth, are
found, alongside pretty gritstone villages. In the north, where the wild moorlands
of Kinder Scout, Bleaklow and Black Hill dominate, the few scattered settlements
seek shelter in the broad dales below.

Bamford *This spirited modern sculpture which stands in the centre of the village of Bamford is one of several which were commissioned by the villagers to mark the Millennium in 2000. It shows Bamford Mill which was built as a cotton mill in 1820 and was later converted to manufacture electrical furnaces. Today it enjoys another life as the provider of high-class living accommodation.*

Bamford *A hazy autumnal morning looking over the village of Bamford from the slopes of Bamford Edge. The spire of the parish church of St John the Baptist is prominent in the foreground, while Shatton and Bradwell Moors fill the skyline in the distance.*

Baslow *A frosty winter's morning at Nether End, Baslow. The bridge, which is now mainly used by walkers entering Chatsworth Park, was originally a narrow packhorse bridge over the Bar Brook, on the old road to Chesterfield. It was later widened to take heavier transport.*

Beeley *Old ivy-clad gritstone cottages at Beeley, one of the Chatsworth estate villages on the southern edge of the Devonshire family's great deer park. Beeley takes its name from a former saxon resident, and means 'Bega's Leah' or clearing.*

Calver *Village post offices, like this one at Calver, and shops are under threat in many parts of the Peak District as a more mobile population uses the surrounding towns and cities for its shopping. Once the shop disappears, it is usually not long before the school is threatened, and the village is in danger of becoming a dormitory.*

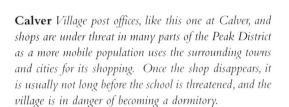

Curbar *Autumn bronzes the bracken below Curbar Edge as the sun lights up the village in the broad valley of the Derwent, with Longstone Edge in the distance. Curbar lies on the eastern bank of the river, with Calver its twin on the western bank.*

Edale *The three-hundred-year-old Old Nag's Head in the centre of Edale village –
more properly known as Grindsbrook Booth – has a special place in the hearts of long-
distance walkers, because it marks the southern terminus of the 270-mile Pennine Way.*

Edale *Edale is actually the name of the valley of the River Noe, and interspersed along it are a series of hamlets known as 'booths' – an old word for cattle shelter. This is Upper Booth, the settlement at the western end of the valley, and it shows how it is enclosed by the highest hills in the Peak.*

Edale *A wintery view of Edale, showing the snowy slopes of Grindslow Knoll (left) and Kinder Scout running away to the right. It is at times like these that the hardy sheep like the Swaledale ram on the left, come into their own, surviving in the harshest of conditions.*

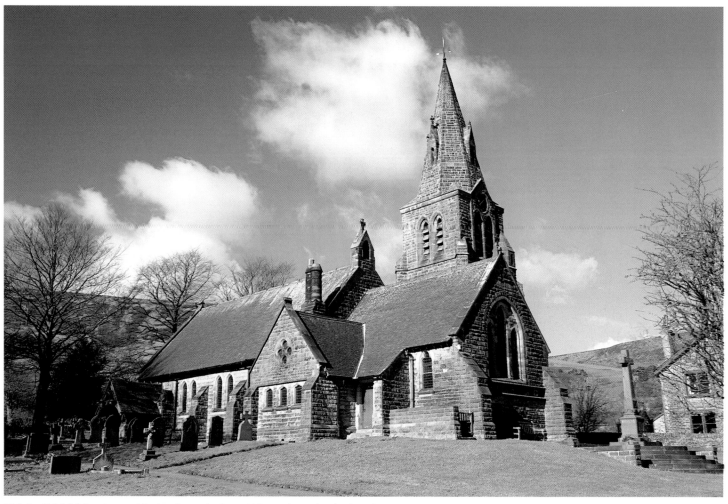

Edale *Edale's Victorian parish church was built in 1886 and was the third on the site. The first church was a great boon to the people of the remote upland valley. Until its construction, they had to take the bodies of their dead on the long trek up the 'corpse road' over Hollin's Cross and down into Castleton for burial.*

Edensor *A glorious autumnal view of the planned village of Edensor from Chatsworth's rolling parklands. Prominent is George Gilbert Scott's St Peter's parish church, built in 1867. The rest of the village was designed in the* cottage ornée *style for the 6th Duke of Devonshire, each cottage being slightly different from the next, but overall creating a pleasing pattern.*

Grindleford *Grindleford's famous ramblers' café has served walkers with great bacon 'sarnies' or 'bangers and mash' for many years. It occupies the old railway station building on the Hope Valley line, near the portals of the 3-mile long Totley Tunnel, which when it opened in 1893 was one of the longest in Britain.*

High and Low Bradfield *Contented cattle enjoy the summer sun in the foreground of this lovely view of High and Low Bradfield, taken from the south. The reason for the qualifying names of the twin village can be clearly seen, as can the ancient tower of High Bradfield's parish church of St Nicholas in the centre of the picture. A glimpse of the Agden Reservoir can just be seen on the extreme left.*

High Bradfield *Bradfield's fifteenth-century parish church has one of the finest views from any Peak District church. It stands on a hill overlooking the Agden Reservoir and the high Bradfield Moors. Another special feature is the Watch House, seen on the left of the photograph, which was built in 1745 to guard against body-snatchers.*

High Bradfield *A good example of how the designation of conservation-area status can improve the environment of a village. This neat example of cobbling, with the Gothic windows of the Watch House in the left background, was executed by the National Park Authority.*

Hathersage *A distant view of Hathersage in the Hope Valley, with Win Hill on the left and Bamford Edge, the prominent escarpment on the left above the village. Hathersage takes its name from Haefer's or heather ridge, a probable reference to the moorland slopes which rise above it.*

Hathersage *A clipped yew shelters the gravestone of Little John, Robin Hood's legendary henchman, in the churchyard of St Michael's at Hathersage. Now adopted by the Ancient Order of the Foresters, the grave is 10-feet long, but there is no conclusive evidence that Little John is buried there, nor even that he ever existed.*

Hathersage *Dramatic late-evening sunshine lights the Tudor tower house of North Lees Hall, above Hathersage, which is reputedly the original for Thornfield Hall in Charlotte Brontë's classic novel,* Jane Eyre. *Charlotte is known to have stayed with her friend Ellen Nussey in Hathersage while she was writing her masterpiece.*

Hayfield *The River Sett winds through the bustling Dark Peak village of Hayfield, on the western slopes of Kinder Scout. The river has played an important part in the history of Hayfield, powering its mills and flooding the town on several occasions, even disinterring corpses from the village churchyard, which adjoins the river.*

Holme *Holme village lies on the northernmost extremity of the Peak District National Park, on the edge of 'Last of the Summer Wine' country. This view shows the village it its idyllic setting, looking south east with a glimpse of Riding Wood Reservoir and Ramsden Clough in the distance.*

Holme *In a scene which could have been taken from the long-lived television comedy series set in nearby Holmfirth, a pair of walkers enjoy one of the many ancient moorland tracks which cross the high Pennines and converge on the village of Holme.*

Holme *Allotments were once an important source of vegetables for Peak District villagers, and many are still in use, like these at Holme. The high moorland of Black Hill forms an impressive backdrop as the villager hoes his soil in preparation for planting.*

Holme *An unusual and stylish farm gate by the side of a ruler-straight enclosure road which leads towards Black Hill and the needle of the Holme Moss television station on the left skyline. Holme Moss transmits TV pictures to much of the northern part of the Peak District.*

Padley *Padley Chapel, actually the former gatehouse of demolished Padley Hall, is the scene of an annual pilgrimage in memory of the Roman Catholic martyrs, Nicholas Garlick and Robert Ludlam, who were executed in 1588 for practising their beliefs. The chapel has a simple, barn-like quality, but is nonetheless an evocative place.*

Padley *Autumn tints the leaves of the beeches and sessile oaks of Padley Gorge, a beautiful and unspoilt wooded clough through which the Burbage Brook runs down from the moors. Padley Gorge is famous for its birdlife, especially the flycatchers − rare summer visitors from Africa.*

Pilsley *The Virginia creeper blushes a bright crimson on the right of this photograph of the Chatsworth estate village of Pilsley, a mile to the west of 'the big house'. As at nearby Edensor, many of the cottages in the village were designed by Joseph Paxton for the 6th Duke.*

Rowsley *Washing day in Rowsley (right). A villager hangs out her colourful washing in this shot taken from the weir across the River Wye near Caudwell's Mill. A craft centre and restaurant are also to be found at Caudwell's, a beautifully-preserved Victorian mill, including a blacksmith's shop (left).*

WESTERN DARK PEAK

The 'Wild West' of the Peak District is characterised by bleak, open moorland punctuated by less regular outcrops of millstone grit than in the east, such as the weird rock formations of The Roaches and Ramshaw Rocks, near Upper Hulme. This is where the Peak District enters Staffordshire and Cheshire, and the few villages are again isolated and tucked away in secret valleys.

Butterton *The elegant needle of the spire of Butterton's parish church of St Thomas, seen here from the south of the village, was built by the Pilkington family in 1845. The village stands high on the White Peak plateau above the River Manifold, and the line of trees near the church marks an igneous intrusion into the predominant limestone.*

Flash *High on the moors to the south of Buxton, Flash lays claim to being the highest village in Britain, standing as it does at 1518 feet above the sea. A tractor was the only traffic on the road which passes between the New Inn and the parish church when the photographer called. Flash was once famous for the production of counterfeit, or 'flash', coins.*

Flash *Winter grips the Staffordshire moorlands south of the village. Only the hardiest of sheep, like the Swaledales shown here, can survive in these semi-Arctic conditions.*

Grindon *The octagonal spire of Victorian Grindon church, known as 'the Cathedral of the Staffordshire Moorlands', is a well-known landmark in the Manifold Valley. Inside is a lesser-known memorial which illustrates the severity of the winters in these parts. In 1947, an RAF Halifax bomber bringing emergency supplies to the isolated community which had been cut off by heavy snowfalls, crashed nearby, killing all eight crew members.*

Hollinsclough *George Mellor has lived in Hollinsclough in the Upper Dove Valley all his life, and to his mind, there's nowhere finer. His village lies under the 'dragon's back' of Chrome Hill near the head of the Dove Valley, one of the finest ridge walks in the Peak District.*

Hollinsclough *The situation of Hollinsclough beneath Chrome Hill can be seen clearly in this photograph which was taken from the south of the village. Chrome (pronounced 'Croom') Hill was formed from hard, erosion-resistant reef limestone laid down 350 million years ago.*

Kettleshulme *In springtime, the green at Kettleshulme is covered with the golden trumpets of daffodils, as shown here. Kettleshulme was originally settled by Norse people – the name means Ketil's holm or island – and it is one of the largest villages in the Cheshire part of the Peak District.*

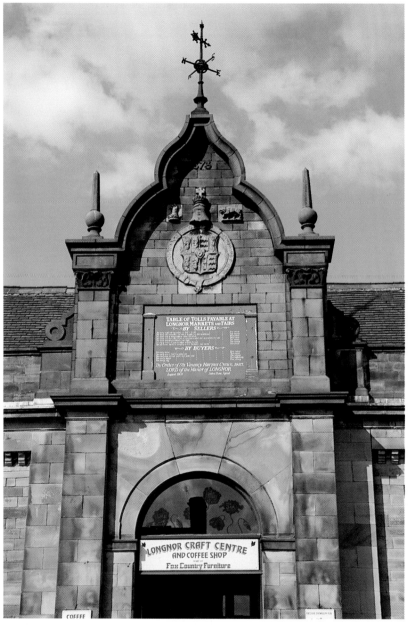

Longnor *The Old Market Hall, built in 1873, in the village square of Longnor still carries the scale of market tolls and charges above its doorway, although it is now a craft centre. Longnor is a prosperous gritstone village standing on a ridge between the limestone dales of the Dove and Manifold.*

Longnor *Cobbled alleyways lead up to St Bartholomew, the parish church of Longnor. Although it is now a sleepy little village, Longnor was once an important market town and, in medieval times, fairs were held in the churchyard.*

Longnor *In the strong light of a late summer's evening, the fields around Longnor take on the appearance of green velvet. In the background can be seen the twin reef limestone peaks of Chrome and Parkhouse Hills, which dominate this part of the Upper Dove Valley.*

Macclesfield Forest *This plain little chapel at Macclesfield Forest retains one of the Peak's oldest customs. At one time, most church floors were covered in rushes or hay which were replaced annually in an act of physical and spiritual renewal. Now Macclesfield Forest is the only one in the Peak District which still performs this ancient ceremony every August.*

Pott Shrigley *This attractive black-and-white half-timbered cottage in the Cheshire village of Pott Shrigley is a real rarity in the Peak District, where stone usually reigns supreme as a building material. Pott Shrigley lies on the westernmost extremity of the Peak District, to the north of Bollington.*

Rainow *A general view of the pretty Cheshire village of Rainow, another on the western edge of the National Park, and the former home of Brian Redhead, broadcaster and ex-president of the Council for National Parks. Rainow gets its name from the Old Norse for 'raven hill'.*

Upper Hulme *More evidence of the Scandinavian influence on the western side of the Peak is found in the Staffordshire village of Upper Hulme, a tiny hamlet which shelters under the bristling escarpment of Hen Cloud, which can just be seen on the left skyline. Hulme is an Old Danish word meaning an island or a piece of land on a stream, in this case the infant River Churnet.*

Upper Hulme *Just north of Upper Hulme lies the jagged ridge of Ramshaw Rocks, seen here in late summer when the heather is in its full glory. Ramshaw Rocks, Hen Cloud and the Roaches form part of the Roaches syncline, and are very popular with rock climbers and scramblers, with fine views across the Cheshire Plain.*

Wetton *Ancient farm machinery left leaning against a flower-decked drystone wall forms an evocative still life in this view from the north of the Staffordshire moorland village of Wetton. In the background, the slopes of Wetton Low rise above the houses of the village.*

Wetton *The sleepy little village of Wetton is the unlikely venue for the even more unlikely World Toe-Wrestling Championships, held here every June. The picture shows contestants hard at it, toe to toe, as they test their toemanship in deadly serious competition.*

Wildboarclough *The Old Post Office in the Cheshire village of Wildboarclough was originally the administrative offices of Crag Mill, an outpost of the silk industry from nearby Macclesfield. When it was still a post office it was reckoned to be one of the largest in the country, ironically serving a tiny community which lives in the shadow of Shutlingsloe.*

Wildboarclough *Seen end on, the shapely ridge of Shutlingsloe (1659 ft) which dominates the village of Wildboarclough is one of the true real 'peaks' in the Peak District. It is also one of its finest viewpoints, with vistas extending over the Lancashire Plain towards the distant River Mersey and the Welsh hills.*

Wincle *For a village so far inland, the name of the Ship Inn in the tiny Cheshire village of Winkle may seem odd. This sixteenth-century red sandstone inn is so named because it commemorates* Nimrod, *the ship used by Ernest Shackleton's 1907 Antarctic expedition, which included Sir Philip Brocklehurst of nearby Swythamley Hall.*